Hello, Boy

Let's play , this special game that I love to SAY

I love to say Hello and I hate to say goodbye

Hello, Hello, Good day
Hello, Hello, I say touch your feet and touch your toes let's say
hello here we go........!

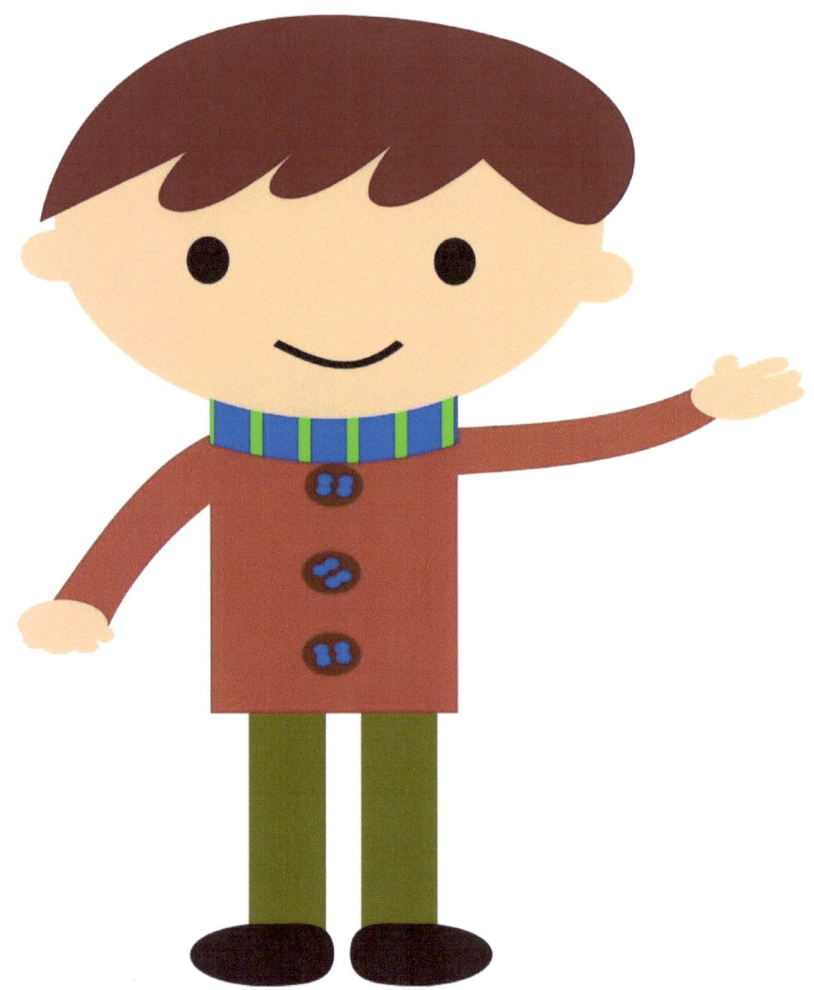

Hello you, hello, me........!

HELLO!

HELLO!

I love to wonder and I love to think

When saying goodbye it really stinks
Hello there let's do a game pick and choose let's say their names

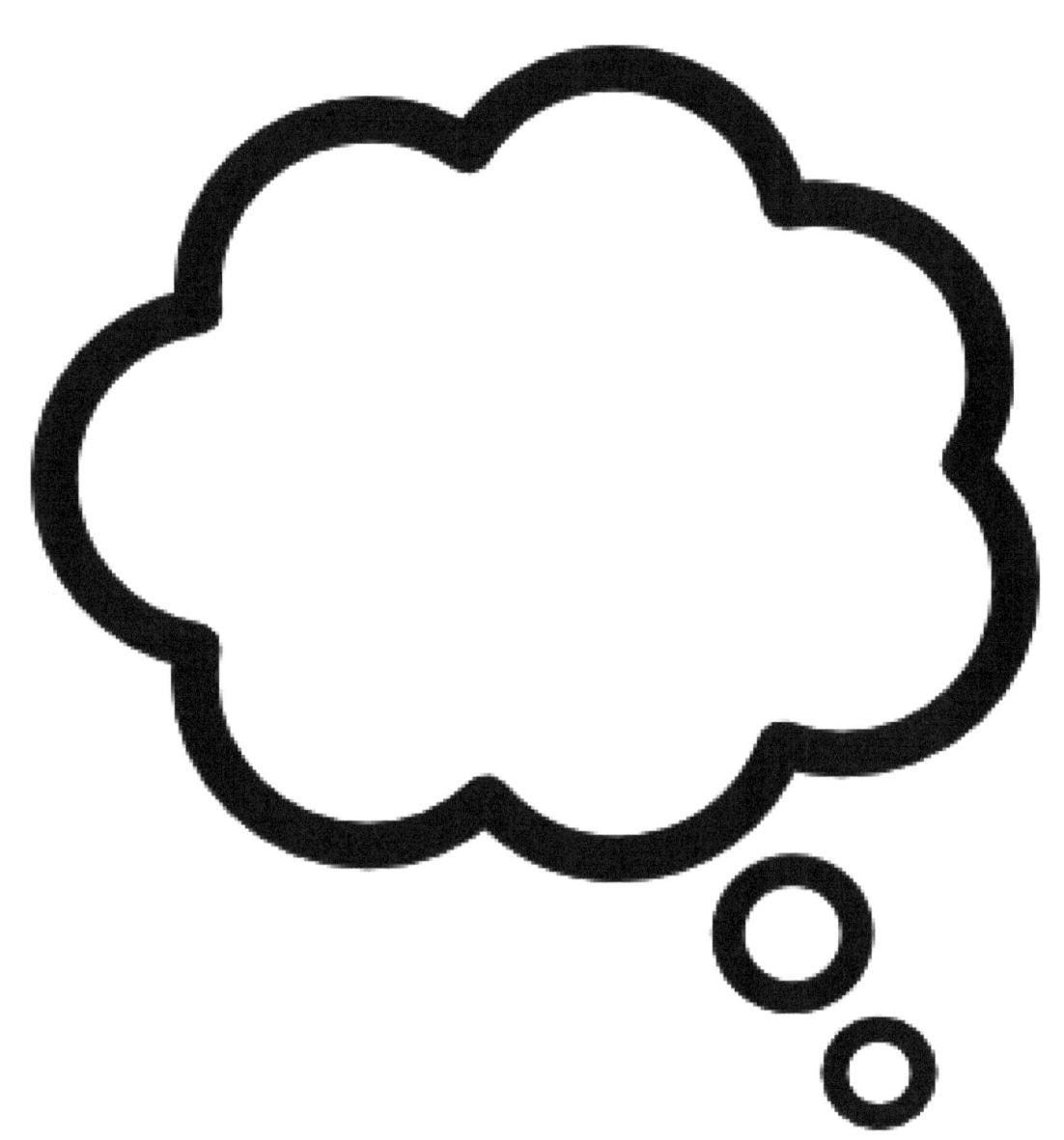

Hello, you, hello me......!

Are you there are you please ?

Listen up I want to play, shout out names and let me say

Hello

Hello

Hello girl,

Hello world I am you and you are her, wave goodbye

And no hello's that's is not the way it goes, I love to think and I

Love to say Hi how are you, how's your day?

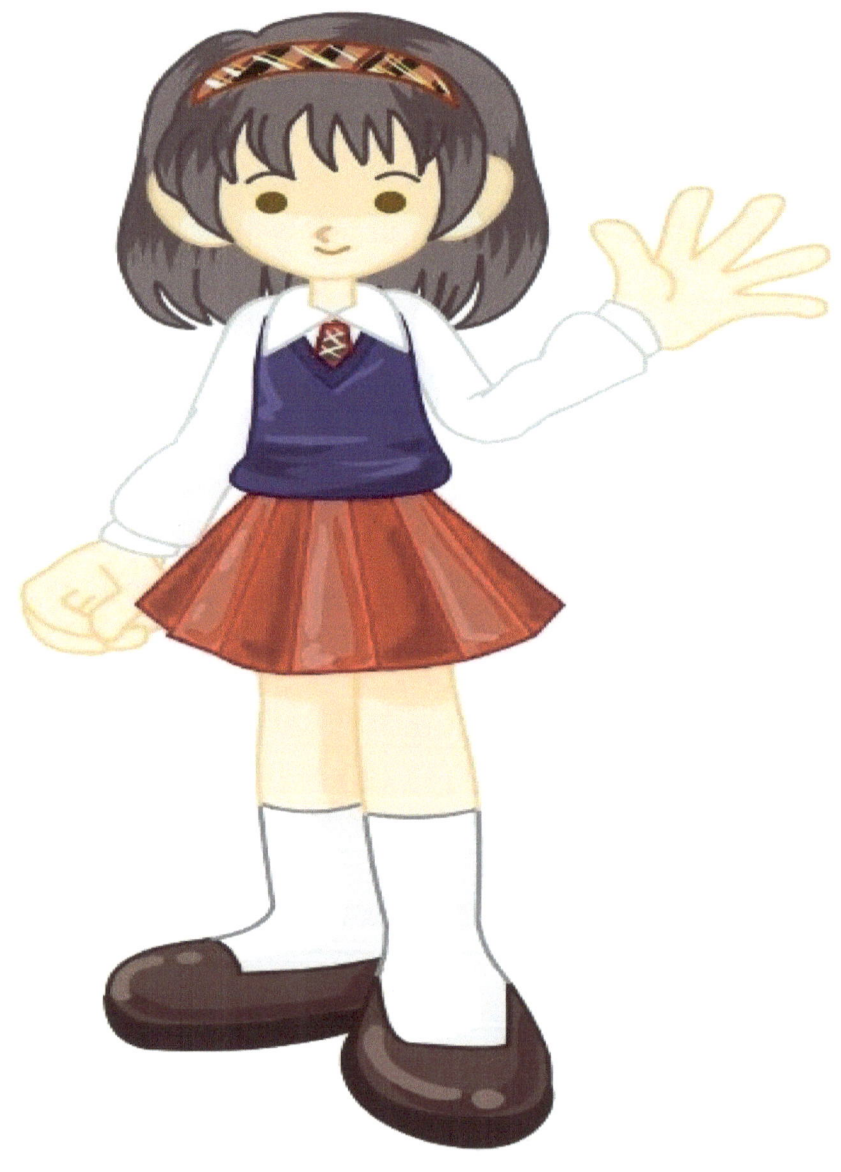

Hello you, hello, me......!

HELLO!

I love to laugh and make a show, wave goodbye and say hello never wonder how it is only know how it feels. It's good to say hello at least you're not alone it's good to say hello then you have a friend.

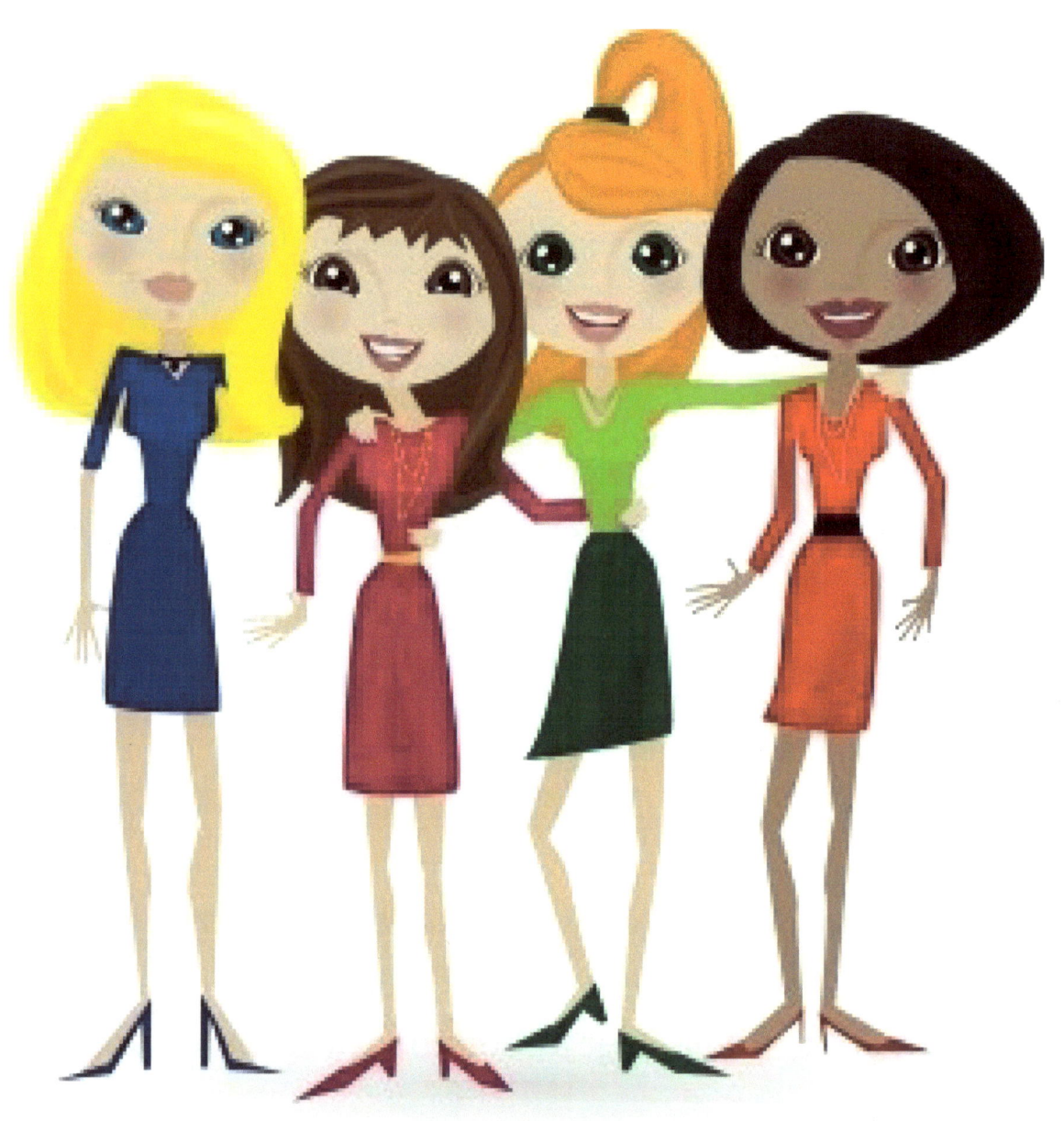

Hello, you, Hello me…….!

Hello!

Let's stay close and put it together Let's go home and bring it together I love to say hello and it's never a goodbye, it's a hi, welcome you , come again, I love you too.

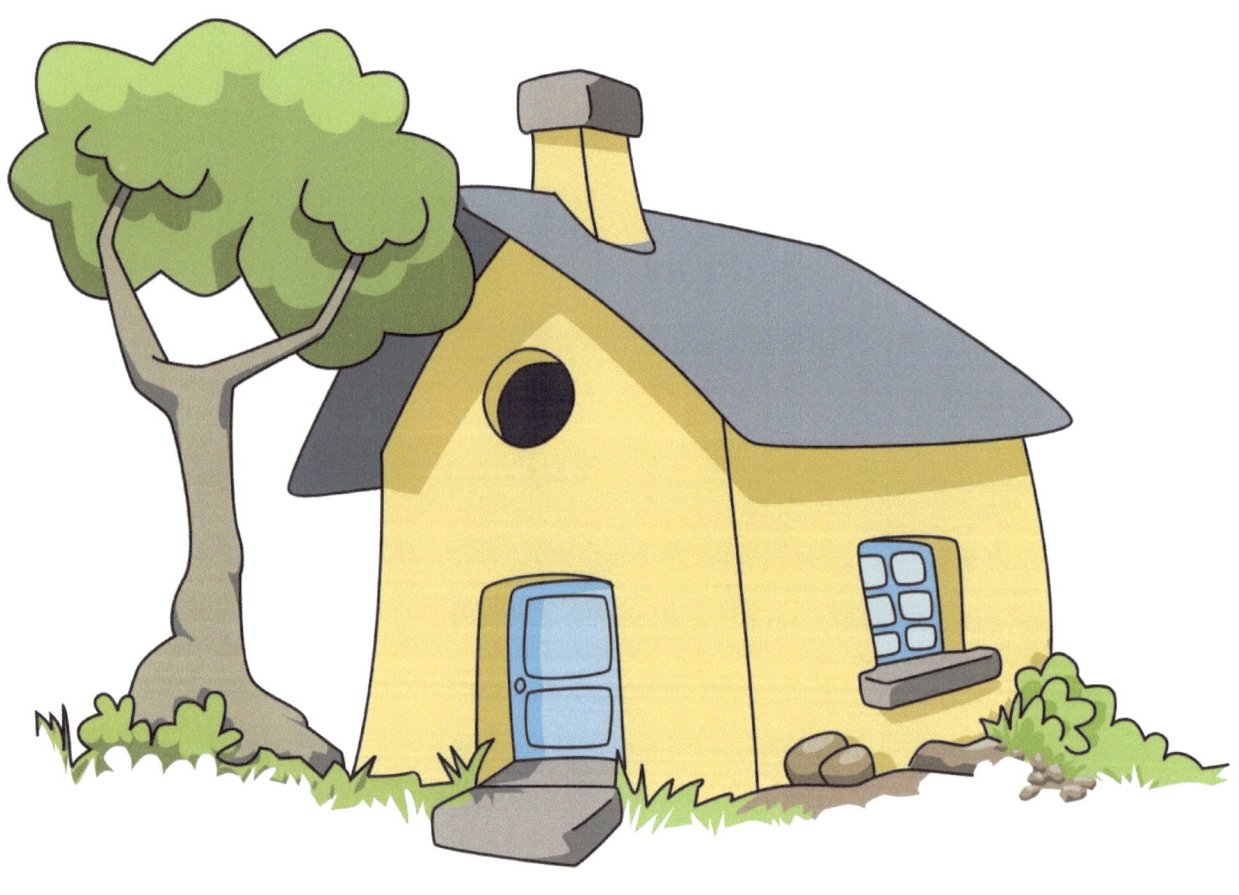

It's almost over and its almost done and you did all the fun by saying hello and saying how do you do now listen closely as this come in two's

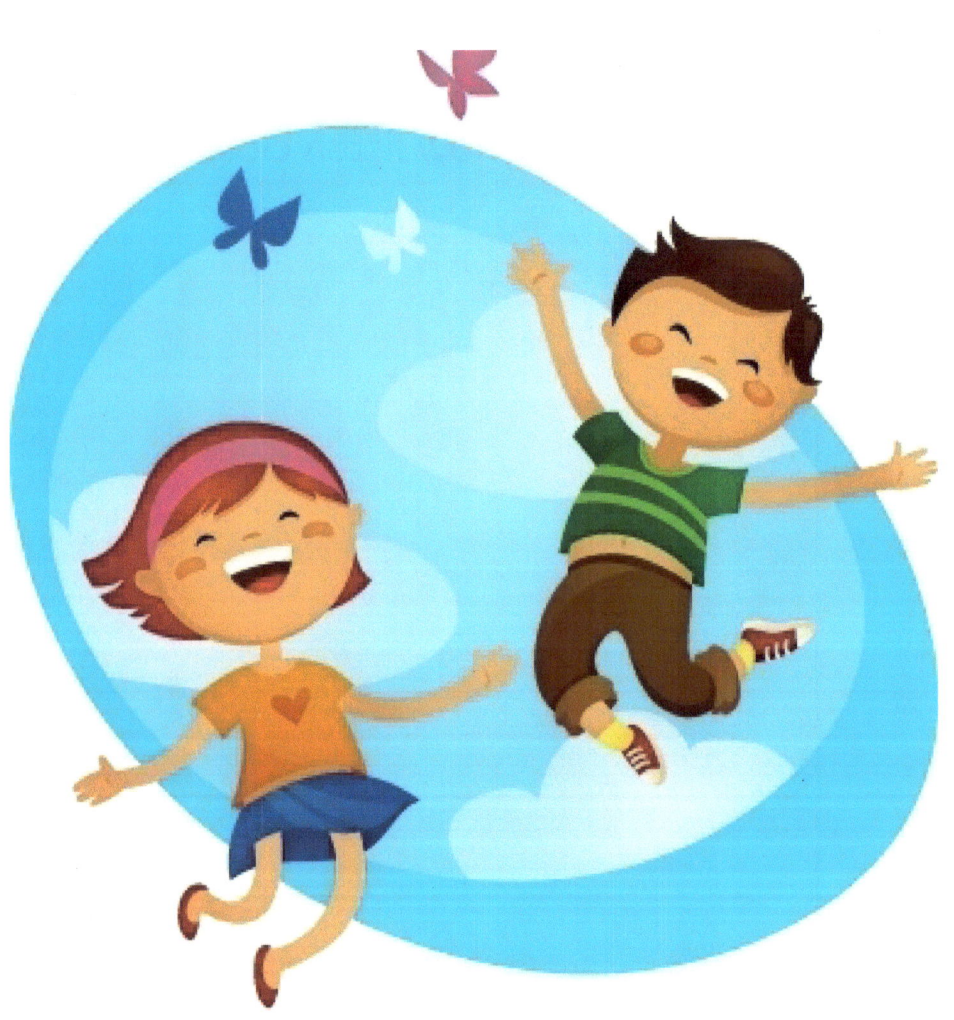

It have to be two in order to meet go have fun go out and see no more hello's it's really time to go no more playing we put on a show and I love to listen and love to think what about you let me see

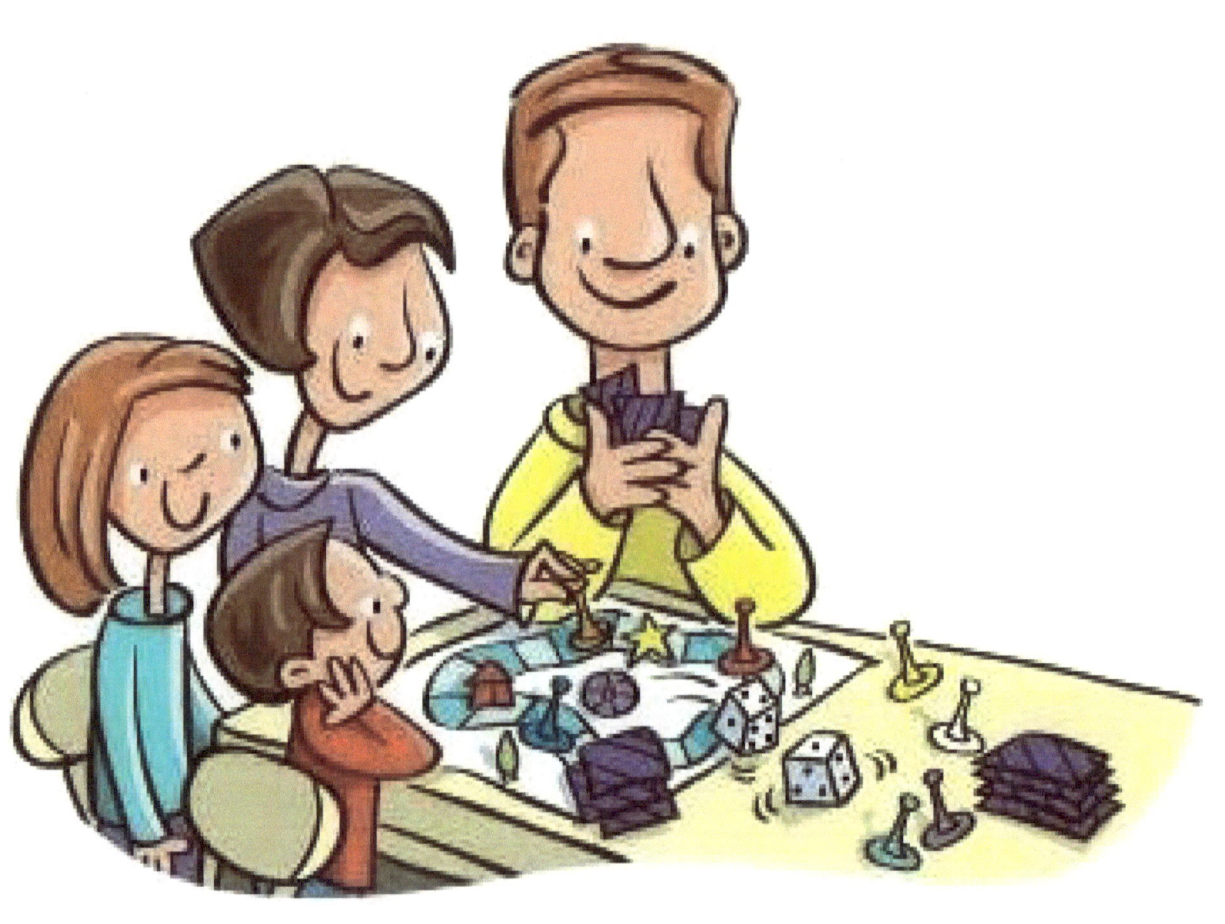

Hello, you, Hello, me, Hello family

Let's all see!

I played this game and I'm very tired we laugh and joke and had fun, it's time to move forward and it's time for a rest, this was just a test, there will always be goodbyes and so many more hello's so here we go….!

Welcome!

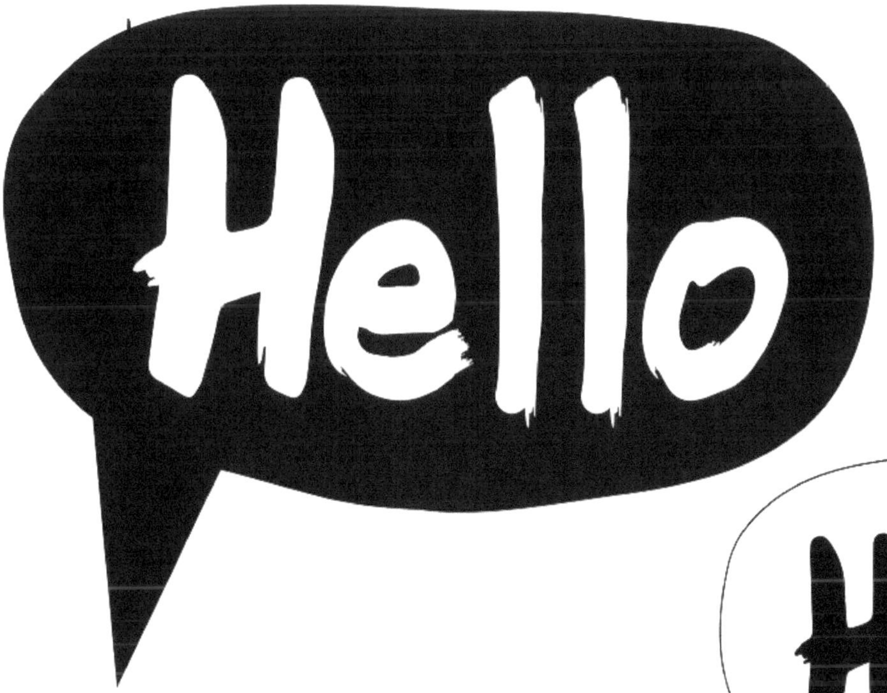
Hello

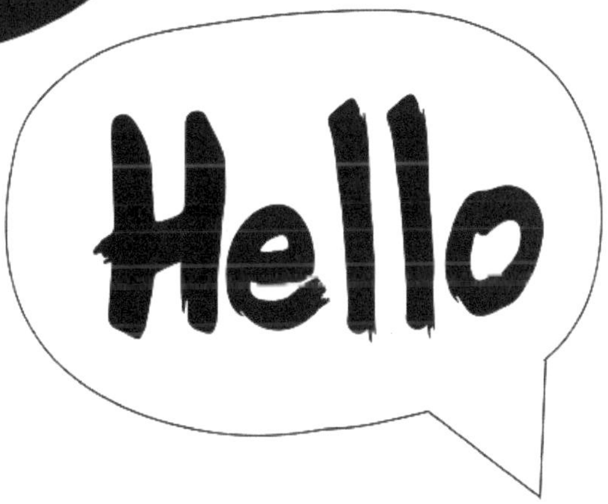
Hello

This story is based on the greeting of hello and the way you acknowledge someone. The way you acknowledge and speak brings wonders to heart and by speaking you are letting the world in every day. So always if you can say Hello, how are you, how's your day, just show respect and say Yes, I'll say hello!

BUT SOMETIMES YOU HAVE TO SAY!

Goodbye

THIS STORY IS THE HELLO STORY

www.ingramcontent.com/pod-product-compliance
Lightning Source LLC
Chambersburg PA
CBHW041310180526
45172CB00003B/1044